THE POWER OF CHOICE

Kristen,

You are the Star!

Sam Silverstein

THE POWER OF CHOICE

Create The Future You Desire
Based On The Choices You Make

SAM SILVERSTEIN

STAR PUBLISHING

ST. LOUIS

Publisher's Cataloging in Publication

Silverstein, Sam
    The power of choice : create the future you desire based on the choices you make /
Sam Silverstein. --St. Louis : Star Pub.,
    1998

        p. cm.

        ISBN 0-9639468-1-1
            1. Choice (Psychology)   2. Decision making.   I. Title.

    BF611 .S55 1998   98-84653
    153.8/3--dc21   CIP

Printed in the United States of America

For Renee, Allison, Geoffrey, Jaclyn, and Sara.

Introduction

We become what we become because of the way we choose and will ourselves to think. Our choices affect our thoughts and our thoughts affect who we are, what we stand for, and the footprints we leave on this planet.

Throughout our lives, we are faced with a myriad of choices. We may not always recognize their presence, but, like it or not, we are constantly faced with the responsibility of choosing. There is no escaping this responsibility. Not deciding what to do or how to act in a given situation is, in itself, a choice.

Some of our choices are simple, like what to wear or what to eat for breakfast. Some carry more importance, like what career we pursue or where we live. Even other choices are life impacting and shape our entire being. These are the choices on which I choose to focus.

Making choices also means accepting the idea that we are part of a bigger picture. We are not alone in our choices. Our choices affect not only ourselves, but the people around us. Our choices shape our actions. Our actions are received and interpreted by those around us. These actions shape the opinions and feelings of those individuals and, ultimately, the actions they take for or against our behalf.

Some choices we make, like our financial well being, will ultimately affect the members of our immediate family. As we grow financially, we are in a position to provide on a different level for those we love. We make choices regarding our values and how we balance our lives. These choices will certainly impact our family and friends. How you treat others professionally will impact the results your business team achieves. As you can see, the choices we make can affect a wide array of people in our lives.

To a great extent, our beliefs about ourselves and our own capabilities, as well as how we see the world and the forces at play in it, affect what we will find possible. These beliefs will impact our choices. Our choices will shape our actions and our actions will determine our results.

Our choices not only affect us today, but affect our abilities and our choices in the future. For instance, if you feel out of control in a given situation, you may choose to withdraw or avoid the problems at hand. This choice leads you to escape from a challenge instead of confronting and possibly overcoming it. The degree to which you avoid or escape from problems today impairs your ability to face, deal with, and grow from various challenges in the future. Choices you make today will prepare you for choices you will be faced with in the future. As the complexity of life evolves, one choice will build on another, enabling you to handle increasingly difficult situations.

An awareness of choice is the first step towards growth. It is critical that we understand the importance of our choices and also the value of the present. By focusing on our current actions, living in the moment, we develop a certain mindfulness and can apply ourselves to do the very best job possible right now! Clarity of mind allows us to recognize the choices at hand and deal with them in a positive and proactive manner.

Some choices are easy to make and others are more difficult. Understanding the possible outcomes helps you make some of those choices. As you read this book, you will notice a choice followed by a clarifying paragraph. In the clarifying paragraph, you will find statements of belief and additional questions. It is not my intention to provide the answers based on my belief system. It is to provide questions that will allow you to probe deeper into your thoughts and feelings.

Many of the choices we face have multiple options. Sometimes we are dealing with right and wrong, but many times there is no wrong answer. The brevity I take in expanding on each choice is by design. It is my goal to assist you in starting the process. You must then accept the responsibility to probe deeper and reach your true inner feelings and desires. You must make these choices for yourself.

It is a journey we all take, building one choice upon another as we grow and prosper. You can create the future you desire based on the choices you make today!

—— Thoughts ——

What do you choose to value?

══════════════════

What is really important to you? Do your actions confirm your placement of value? So often we say that one thing is important, but we find ourselves caught up with other projects. Defining what you value is important. Spending your time pursuing your defined values is critical to both happiness and a high level of achievement.

—— Thoughts ——

D o you use vision to create the future, or are you blind to the possibilities?

━━━━━━━━━━━━━━

Life is a self-fulfilling prophesy. What you see in your future will drive your actions today. It is those actions that determine what you achieve. By opening your mind to the possibilities, you enable your mind to create a vision filled with your desired achievements. This new expanded vision of your future will drive you to do what is necessary today to arrive at the future you create.

—— Thoughts ——

D o you choose to say "can do" or "can't do"?

―――――――――

Your attitude affects your actions and your actions affect your results. A positive attitude will allow you to apply yourself until you achieve the results you desire.

—— Thoughts ——

Do you accept the circumstances you were born into or do you evaluate them and choose to change them if necessary?

Many people accept their lot in life based on the socioeconomic environment into which they were born. Your position in life is not cast in stone based on your parents' position. You can educate yourself and, through hard work, move to any level you truly desire. The choice is yours.

—— Thoughts ——

A re you going to balance the areas of your life or neglect important issues and needs?

━━━━━━━━━━

Do you balance business and family? Does one area of your life suffer because of imbalance? Are you able to prioritize your interests and objectives and then stick to your hierarchy of needs? By balancing the major areas of your life, you create an inner harmony. The seven areas in which to seek balance are career/financial, family, health, social, education, recreation, and spiritual. Happiness is attained by achieving success in all of the major areas of your life. Balance means recognizing that you have a variety of needs and working towards fulfilling those needs.

—— Thoughts ——

Do you choose to live with virtue or with disdain for righteousness?

――――――

Someone who lives with moral excellence and right-eousness understands the order of life. Unwritten principles dictate that true success and happiness do not come from impure thoughts or actions. Through kindness in attitude and actions you grow as an indi-vidual and increase your personal power. Virtuous living will create enormous power. The virtue you display will attract others like a magnet, and they, in turn, will work toward the achievement of your goals.

— **Thoughts** —

Do you respect others?

━━━━━━━━━━━━━━━━

By honoring others, you honor yourself. Respect for others is translated into empowerment of others. Empowered people achieve excellence. While not necessarily your goal, many times the excellence that others achieve will bring you positive rewards in the process. Respect for others is a supreme compliment.

—— Thoughts ——

D o you respect yourself?

Respect for yourself means nurturing, protecting and empowering your mental and physical being. It means understanding that you have needs that must be met to be your best and that you must seek to fulfill those needs. By respecting yourself, you can then respect others. Do you place your well-being on a pedestal? Do you provide yourself with the nurturing necessary to grow and flourish?

—— **Thoughts** ——

Do you keep life's issues in perspective or overreact and waste time on meaningless events?

━━━━━━━━━━━━━━

Do you keep your head about you? Are your decisions based solely on emotion or is rational thinking involved? Do the little issues get in the way of the big ones? Many times keeping life in perspective means being able to step "outside" of yourself and look back at your situation with less emotion. What advice would you give someone else in a similar situation? Does this "uninvolved" advice make sense for you?

—— Thoughts ——

Do you get to go to work or have to go to work?

Is your job your chore or your passion? If you are passionate about what it is you do, you will find yourself producing superior results. A happy work environment sends you home happy. Most people work the majority of their grown lives. What could you accomplish if your job was your passion? Shouldn't your job be your passion?

—— Thoughts ——

Do you live with humility, or are you vain and arrogant?

━━━━━━━━━━━━

To grow and achieve, it is important to place your focus on your vision and your goals. By always looking for credit, you falsely build yourself up at the expense of others. By living a humble life you build up others who, in turn, will look to assist you and help you achieve your goals.

—— Thoughts ——

Do you choose to love or be bogged down in hate and degrading emotions?

———————

Do the important people in your life know how you feel about them? Relationships are based on communication. Great communication leads to great relationships. Are you able to forgive and move on? When someone treats you poorly, how does that affect your actions? Holding grudges means holding on to and focusing on past negative events. Most times this comes at a cost of losing focus of your vision. The grudge garners your attention. The vision is lost.

—— Thoughts ——

Do you live with courage or in constant fear?

———————————

Fear of failure and fear of the unknown get in the way of many people's successes. People who are "frozen" by fear do not do what is necessary to achieve what it is they are seeking. If you let fear negatively affect your actions, you are condemning yourself to failure through inactivity. Are you able to control your fears or do they control you? Do you let anything stand in your way of achieving what you are seeking?

—— Thoughts ——

Are you willing to do what you have to do until you get to do what you want to do?

————————————

There are no overnight successes. What appears to be instant success is usually many months and even years of dedicated work that has built up to eventual success. Don't look for instant gratification. Recognize that if you work hard at what has to be done you will reap the rewards and get to where you want to be.

—— Thoughts ——

Will you show responsibility in your actions or live with immaturity?

―――――――――――――

Some decisions are difficult. Can you make the tough choice? When you make a commitment to someone, do you keep it? When you make a commitment to yourself, do you keep it? Do you fulfill all of your obligations, both pleasant and unpleasant?

— Thoughts —

Do you strive to develop competence, or are you willing to accept mediocrity?

Developing competence--being excellent in your talents and abilities--means building the skills and techniques necessary to perform at a high level. Great athletes develop competence. Great leaders develop competence. Great parents develop competence. In what areas do you need to develop greater competence? What are you doing on a daily basis to develop that competence?

—— Thoughts ——

A re you going to treat education as a continuing and ongoing pursuit, or are you going to neglect the growth of your mental capacity?

The world is changing at a rapid pace. What are you doing to keep up with advancements in technology and information? Knowledge creates value. Expanding your knowledge base expands and increases your value to your career, value to your family, and value to yourself. Education opens new doors. As you expand your thinking, you expand your possibilities. Do you have a consistent and ongoing plan for continuing education?

—— Thoughts ——

A re you going to choose to achieve financial freedom or live a life of dependency and want?

_____

As children we are used to others providing for us. As adults we must provide for ourselves and, in many cases, our families. What are you doing to position yourself to provide superior financial stability? What level of financial ability is necessary to make you happy? Are you achieving that level? If not, why?

—— Thoughts ——

Is honesty the backbone of your actions and statements, or do you willingly deceive?

━━━━━━━━━━━━

What do you stand for? Is your word your bond? For what actions are you known? Many times people find it difficult to be honest. How do you handle those situations? Do you choose the easy way out?

—— Thoughts ——

Do you take care of your body and strive to be fit, or do you let health issues reduce your effectiveness and ability to live life to the fullest?

We are only given one vehicle with which to navigate our world. What are you doing to maintain your vessel? If you achieve financial freedom, will you be able to physically enjoy your successes? What steps can you take to improve your level of physical fitness?

—— Thoughts ——

Do you focus on the needs of others, or are you only concerned with your own self-interests?

═══════════════

How important is the success of those around you? Do you spend time helping others achieve success? Helping others is a reward in and of itself. And in the end, you may find that by helping other people achieve their goals, they may be willing to help you achieve yours.

—— Thoughts ——

Do you prejudge or let people and issues stand on their own merit?

───────────────

One of the main reasons many salespeople fail is that they prejudge whether a customer can or will buy. Does someone's clothes really tell if he or she is financially capable of making a purchase? What opportunities might you be passing up by prejudging the outcome? Do you give people a fair opportunity to produce positive results?

—— Thoughts ——

Do you live with prejudice or acceptance?

Does sex, race or creed really make a difference in someone's ability to perform a certain task? How do you treat people? If you were the minority, how would you like to be treated? Do your actions and statements affirm your beliefs of equality?

—— **Thoughts** ——

Do you develop and protect your self-esteem or neglect it?

Your self-esteem limits or enhances your ability to achieve. If you look at yourself as a loser, it is impossible to be a winner. If you have a good, healthy self-image, you will have a greater will and ability to succeed. People with good self-images better understand the relationship between their optimal selves and their actual selves and are constantly striving to achieve their higher potential. How do you see yourself? What can be done to strengthen your self-esteem? If you had a stronger self-esteem, what would you be able to accomplish?

—— Thoughts ——

A re your actions consistent with your words, or do you act hypocritically?

━━━━━━━━━━
━━━━━━━━━━

Many times it is easy to say what is right. Do your actions agree with your statements? Do you walk your talk or do you say one thing and do another? Do you expect more from others than from yourself? When your actions are aligned with your words, you gain credibility. People believe in what you say and are more likely to assist you as you pursue your goals. As your deeds come in line with your words, you will notice a significant increase in your productivity and level of achievement.

—— Thoughts ——

Will you have a healthy diet or ignore what your body needs to operate efficiently?

―――――――――――

Just as a high performance engine needs a high octane fuel, your body needs the right food to operate efficiently. You wouldn't put cheap fuel in a race car or a jet airplane. You wouldn't feed expensive show dogs table scraps. Treat your body with respect. Eat the right food, and you will see your energy level grow. As your energy grows, your mental capacity and your ability to excel grows. Leave the competition at the starting line. Eat high performance, and achieve high performance.

—— Thoughts ——

Do you choose to let your ego govern your words and actions, or do you keep it in check?

When success comes your way, who gets the credit? Are you preoccupied with gaining recognition, or is it results you desire? If you spend your time building up those around you, giving them credit for team achievements and allowing them to feel good, you will achieve more and be in a position to enjoy your successes. By seeking recognition, you may stymie your results. By seeking results, you will probably gain recognition in the process.

—— Thoughts ——

A re you good?

Do your actions portray you as good? Do people want to associate with you because of who you are and what you stand for? Do you look to do good things for others? People are naturally attracted to others with similar values. Which value do you choose? Surrounding yourself with good people will lead to positive outcomes.

—— Thoughts ——

Do you look for and appreciate beauty or choose the bland and mundane?

Beauty surrounds us. Nature offers much beauty. We have an endless availability of "arts" to see and experience. By focusing on beauty, you expand your view of the world around you. By seeking beauty, you expand your vision and the possibilities in your life expand. Seeking beauty is both positive and rewarding. Always look to the beauty, and let it inspire your creative self.

—— **Thoughts** ——

Do you choose to be generous, or are you selfish?

─────────────

Are you always looking to receive? Do you look to give first or take? It's an unwritten law that you cannot take more than you give. A successful society is built on people giving to others. You may not receive back from those you give to, but it *will* come back. The more you give, the more that will come back. Helping others achieve their success will prove to not only be rewarding, but you will grow in the process. As you grow, you will find yourself closer to your goals.

—— Thoughts ——

Do you choose to live in the past, or do you let go of prior problems and failures?

The past is gone. We cannot affect anything that has come before this time. The future inspires our actions today and gives us the energy to do what we must to reach our futures. The present is where we take action and achieve results. If we dwell on past failures, we lose sight of our vision and our goals. When that happens, the source of our energy today is gone, and we stray off course. Learn from the past. Don't live there. Look to the future. Draw energy from the vibrant picture you paint of what it is you desire, and do today whatever it takes to achieve that vision.

—— **Thoughts** ——

Do you choose to be happy with what you have, or do you want for wanting's sake?

━━━━━━━━━━━━━━

Many times people are so driven to *have*, they don't stop to ask *why*. If you just want for wanting's sake, you will never achieve true fulfillment and happiness, no matter what you achieve or attain. If, on the other hand, you understand the value of what you are achieving, you will bring pleasure and happiness to every day of your life.

—— Thoughts ——

A re you kind and do nice things for others, or do you choose indifference?

———

Whose day have you made today? What kind deed have you done? What positive outcome will occur because of your empowering compliment or act? How will your actions affect the success or happiness of others?

—— Thoughts ——

Do you trust others?

———————————

Showing trust empowers people. Empowered individuals are able to accomplish more, both on their own behalf and yours. By trusting others, you put them in a position to show trust in you. That, in turn, empowers you.

—— Thoughts ——

Do you trust yourself?

———

Do you have confidence in your abilities? Do you trust yourself to make good decisions? If you educate yourself and train yourself in the areas you pursue, you will be equipped to make good choices. By having confidence in your actions, showing trust in yourself and your tactics, you empower yourself to focus on the task at hand. This single minded focus will translate into positive results.

— Thoughts —

Do you choose to control your temperament or do you let external events and other people control your emotions?

━━━━━━━━━━━━━━━

Maintaining emotional balance means lowering stress in your life. It also means keeping control and being in a position to make better decisions. Uncontrolled emotions lead to rash and unfounded actions. If you allow others to control your emotions, they will control your actions and, therefore, your results. By controlling your emotions, you maintain full control of your actions and the results you achieve as you move toward attaining your vision.

—— Thoughts ——

Do you choose the easy way out?

Excelling in your professional and personal life means being able to face tough situations and make tough choices. It is tempting to take the easy way out when the good decision is often the one that seemingly requires more effort. What appears tough at the onset may, over time, prove to produce the better results and, ultimately, provide an easier, more comfortable path for you. Tough decisions and a road of quality work often pave the way to a place of success and fulfillment.

—— Thoughts ——

Do you choose to set goals, or do you live adrift?

Goals are the targets of life. Without them, you go through each day without direction. With goals, you supercharge your every minute and every hour. Goals lead to superior planning and superior results. However, creating a vision to which we are striving does not mean to be bound to every step of the way. Do not be afraid to reevaluate your goals and intentions along the way. Remember, very specifically written goals become magnets to which you will find yourself uncontrollably attracted.

—— Thoughts ——

Do you do the job right the first time?

Many times people do not feel they have the time to do their best work. However, they end up having to redo the job or backtrack. If you make it a habit to do great work, you will find your investment in time, money, and credibility will be a lot less than if you have to do the job over.

—— Thoughts ——

H **ave you tapped your natural creativity, or do you choose to allow sameness to limit your opportunities?**

Creativity is the ability to generate new and innovative answers to questions or solutions to problems that, when implemented, will move you closer to realizing your vision of the future. Creativity is an ability that all of us share. The difference between individuals who display creativity and those who don't is the ability to encourage creative impulses and then take action on creative thoughts. Creative thoughts are only beneficial when evaluated and implemented. By asking questions, exposing yourself to a continuous flow of thoughts and ideas, and allowing this input to incubate, you will find yourself generating your own creative ideas and solutions.

—— Thoughts ——

A re you gracious?

By treating others with kindness and courtesy, they will feel appreciated for who they are and the contributions they make. This, in turn, will empower them to do more and give more. As others around you give more, you will naturally receive more and, therefore, achieve more. Acting graciously towards others is not only a display of kindness, but also it helps create an an ever expanding circle of people who will want to assist you and work on your behalf.

—— Thoughts ——

Do you accept responsibility for your achievements and your outcome in life?

———

Are you always looking for shortcuts? Do you believe that others are luckier than you? Is there a magic formula for the success you are seeking? Future results are based on present actions. You are responsible for your actions and, therefore, your results. Taking responsibility for your success is the first step on your road to greatness.

—— Thoughts ——

Do you remove negativity from your life?

Do you bathe yourself with negative thoughts? Are you negative to those around you? Do you find yourself surrounded by others that insist on being negative about either their lives or yours? Negative attitudes and statements drain your life's energy. Each negative statement, by either yourself or someone else, draws energy from you. Energy is critical to work and production. Reduce or eliminate your negative thoughts and work to surround yourself with people who are positive and give you energy rather then those who are negative and take your energy.

—— Thoughts ——

Do you choose to use the opportunity of change as an avenue to growth, or do you reject change and its potential?

Change is the essence of progress. Change is a gift and an opportunity. Through change, you have the opportunity to grow and prosper. Sameness is the enemy of us all. Resisting change is negative. It derails your focus and drains your energy. By tapping your creative powers and embracing change, you envelope yourself with a force that will foster and nourish your growth.

—— Thoughts ——

Do you choose to stand up for your convictions and beliefs, or do you give in to peer pressure?

———————

How strong is your character? Are you able to stay your course when others around you condemn your ideas and display negativity? Can you live with what you want and what you believe is right even when it is not the popular view? Do you make your own decisions, or do you allow others to decide your fate for you?

—— **Thoughts** ——

Do you live your life with passion?

―――――――――

Passion is the seed of all success. It is the foundation for every accomplishment. Passion is the energy that it takes to implement your plans, achieve your goals, and enjoy success. Passion fuels desire. Your level of passion will dictate your level of success. Passion is contagious. Your passion will be mirrored by those around you, and everyone will achieve more. It is unyielding, ever flowing, and always there to call upon.

— **Thoughts** —

D o you choose to use patience?

The Canadian Campion Moss takes twenty years to bear blooms. It takes a certain amount of time for a cake to rise. Rushing the process will only ruin the cake. Patience doesn't mean not caring. It means taking an appropriate action while understanding that process takes time. Patience means allowing the needed amount of time to pass in order for natural events to mature and success to happen. It doesn't mean not pushing ahead with vigor. It just means you realize there can be a set of steps you must pass through as you move to the top.

—— Thoughts ——

A re you compassionate?

Everyone needs a hand now and then. Everyone appreciates a kind word. A genuine care of and for others translates into words and actions. People need to hear words of praise and see your feelings, as displayed in actions. Action on your part validates your words. Sincere concern, appreciation and care are enormously empowering for the recipient, as well as the giver.

—— Thoughts ——

Do you choose to learn from others, or do you feel you know everything you need to know?

―――――――――

In this world, there are three types of knowledge: that which you know, that which you know you don't know and that which you don't know you don't know. The latter is threefold larger in volume than the first two together. Learning what you need to learn will greatly speed up your journey toward success. Vicarious learning, learning from others, is the least expensive way to learn anything. Learning from someone who has achieved the results you desire will greatly shorten your learning curve and increase your staying power as you move toward your goals.

—— Thoughts ——

Do you choose to build up those around you or tear them down?

―――――――――――――

It's quite simple. Putting people down in order to build yourself up is counter productive for both you and them. Demeaning others will not be a positive boost to your self-esteem. You are limiting your allies and your support. Building other people up will help them achieve at a higher level, and they, in turn, will be in a position to help others. Maybe you!

—— Thoughts ——

D o you choose peace or war?

_____

War brings destruction. As troops move into action, they trample everything in their way. Even in victory, the land is destroyed and lives are lost. As you move toward your vision, do you wage war with competitors and associates? Are you destroying someone else's vision or even your own vision? Are you eliminating bridges that connect you to others and their assistance? Peace builds lasting relationships and allows everyone to flourish. War or peace? It's your choice.

—— Thoughts ——

A re you braggadocios, or do you choose to be modest?

Do you choose to achieve for what it represents and what it allows you to enjoy, or do you achieve so others can witness your accomplishments? Are you more concerned with your outcomes or your notoriety? Is success enough even in obscurity? Is it the process and the outcome or the fame? Will chasing fame remove your focus? Can you thrive on results?

—— Thoughts ——

H ave you chosen to use self-discipline, or do you allow yourself to overindulge?

———————————

Can you control your emotions? Can you control your actions? Do you build your character by making tough decisions? Are you training and developing your mental being just as athletes train and develop their physical beings? Can you forgo current pleasure for future gain? Can you do without in order to do with?

—— Thoughts ——

Do you prioritize the interests in your life, or do you jump from endeavor to endeavor and never complete meaningful objectives?

――――――――――

Is there order to your actions? Can you decide what is most important, more important, important and so on as you move toward your goals? Do unimportant activities get in the way of critical activities and goals? Do you take care of the significant issues in your life so you can move on to less meaningful ones? Prioritizing adds power to your actions and greatly enhances your ability to achieve at a very high level.

—— Thoughts ——

Do you have a hero?

Who? Why? What does your hero stand for? Does your hero represent who you are or what you are trying to achieve? Does your hero have similar values as you or is it just his/her achievements that attract you? Worship of others is not healthy. Inspiration from others who have solid beliefs and admirable traits can be very positive.

—— Thoughts ——

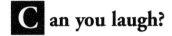 an you laugh?

Do you laugh? When? How seriously do you take yourself? Can you laugh at past mistakes? Laughter is therapeutic. Laughing enables you to release situational tensions and empowers you. Laughter can help you handle embarrassing or difficult situations. Using laughter is one way to maintain control of your emotions. And, you will find, laughter is contagious.

—— Thoughts ——

Do you choose to listen to others, or do you always have to talk?

Do you learn more from speaking or listening? Do you control the conversation? Can you listen more than you talk? Do you express your opinion to satisfy your ego or to contribute to the conversation and move it towards solving issues and providing new information? Are you telling or learning?

—— **Thoughts** ——

How do you choose to be known?

―――――――――――――

When your name is mentioned, what words follow? Are you known for your deeds, achievements, efforts, and contributions? Are positive words used to describe you? Would you want to know what is said? Are you happy with how you are known? If not, what must you do to change? How will you be known next year? What must you do?

—— Thoughts ——

Do you choose to control your thoughts, or do you let your thoughts control you?

━━━━━━━━━━

Your mind can only process one thought at a time. Additionally, your mind cannot tell the difference from a real event and a vividly imagined one. Do you control your thoughts? Do you shape your thoughts to lead you to specific, positive outcomes? Do you keep the key to the gate of your mind? Can you keep negative thoughts out and foster those thoughts that will empower you to greatness?

It's Your Choice

From the moment we are born we are faced with choices. Ultimately, we can choose to succeed or we can choose to fail. Not choosing will usually lead to mediocrity or worse.

Good decisions are based on education, quality information, and a personal commitment to the positive outcome you desire. Success comes from defining the decisions you need to make, making those quality choices, and then taking action on your decisions.

Positive results and success do not always show themselves at once. In fact, sometimes we must experience hardship and negative results in order to learn, build, and make better choices. Failure only comes from quitting and denying the process the time necessary to evolve into success.

Every day you are faced with decisions and alternatives. Your successes and ultimate greatness is up to you. It's based on your vision, the way you think, and the choices you make. Greatness is available to you. **It's your choice.**

About The Author

Sam Silverstein has a solid track record in building million dollar dreams. The numbers speak for themselves. He has sold over 100 million dollars of products and services. Mr. Silverstein earned his Bachelor of Business Administration at the University of Georgia and his Masters in Business Administration from Washington University. Mr. Silverstein is a member of the National Speakers Association. As president of Sam Silverstein Enterprises, Inc., Mr. Silverstein speaks internationally on the topics of personal and professional empowerment and helps organizations become more effective in managing change, learning leadership skills, creative marketing, and solution based selling techniques.

Additionally, Mr. Silverstein is active in civic organizations and is an avid marathoner. He and his wife, Renee, have four children and live in a suburb of St. Louis.

Also By Sam Silverstein
The Success Model™

For more information on Sam Silverstein keynote presentations, training seminars, audio cassette albums, books, and consulting services, call or write:

SAM SILVERSTEIN ENTERPRISES, INC.
121 Bellington   Suite 400
St. Louis, Missouri 63141
888•668•4828
www.samsilverstein.com